My Secret
Fantasies

My Secret Fantasies

THE LOVERS' BOOK OF SHARING KATE F. MOORE

STERLING/RAVENOUS
An imprint of Sterling Publishing Co., Inc.

New York / London
www.sterlingpublishing.com

10 9 8 7 6 5 4 3 2 1

Produced by Ravenous
An imprint of Hollan Publishing, Inc.
100 Cummings Center, Suite 125G
Beverly, MA 01915
www.hollanpub.com

© 2008 by Hollan Publishing, Inc.

Published by Sterling Publishing Co., Inc.
387 Park Avenue South, New York, NY 10016

Distributed in Canada by Sterling Publishing
c/o Canadian Manda Group, 165 Dufferin Street
Toronto, Ontario, Canada M6K 3H6
Distributed in the United Kingdom by GMC Distribution Services
Castle Place, 166 High Street, Lewes, East Sussex, England BN7 1XU
Distributed in Australia by Capricorn Link (Australia) Pty. Ltd.
P.O. Box 704, Windsor, NSW 2756, Australia

Printed in China

Sterling ISBN-13: 978-1-4027-5534-7
        ISBN-10: 1-4027-5534-1

For information about custom editions, special sales, premium and corporate purchases, please contact Sterling Special Sales Department at 800-805-5489 or specialsales@sterlingpublishing.com.

Production design by Susan Raymond

Contents

Introduction

*F*ewer than 50 years ago, sexual fantasies were seen by many "experts" as a form of deviancy, and some disputed the notion that women had sexual fantasies at all. Now almost everyone in our culture acknowledges fantasy as a fun, healthy way for both you and your partner to explore your sexuality, learn about your personal pleasure centers, expand your boundaries, and, yes, pass the time while you wait at the grocery store.

This book is a way for you to continue that fantasy exploration. Think about your old favorites, expand on a current fantasy, or maybe give something you haven't thought of a spin. Then, if you're feeling bold, you might even hand this book to your partner . . . Who knows what will turn up?

Wishing you many happy days and nights.

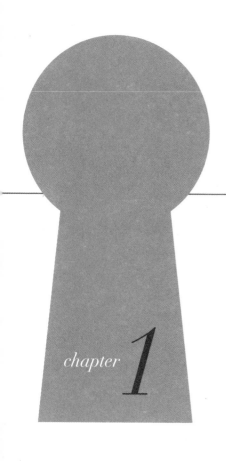

Warming Up

chapter *1*

The Reality of the Situation

In real life, I'm most likely to . . .

☐ be seduced ☐ be the seducer
☐ be both seduced *and* the seducer

When I fantasize, I'm most likely to . . .

☐ be seduced ☐ be the seducer ☐ it's about even

My fantasies are usually . . .

☐ more about making a physical connection
☐ more about making an emotional connection
☐ about making both a physical and emotional connection

When I have sex in real life, I focus more on . . .

☐ making a physical connection
☐ making an emotional connection
☐ making both a physical and emotional connection

My fantasies usually involve more elaborate seduction than in real life.

☐ true ☐ false

My fantasies usually involve more foreplay than in real life.

☐ true ☐ false

My fantasies usually involve more intercourse than in real life.

☐ true ☐ false

My fantasies usually involve giving more oral sex than in real life.

☐ true ☐ false

My fantasies usually involve receiving more oral sex than in real life.

☐ true ☐ false

My fantasies usually involve more anal sex than in real life.

☐ true ☐ false

In my fantasies, I usually have . . .

☐ more slow, sensual sex ☐ more quickies
☐ rougher sex ☐ gentler sex

In my fantasies . . .

☐ naked is sexier ☐ clothed is sexier

My favorite fantasy position is . . .

☐ me on top ☐ my partner on top ☐ side-by-side ☐ standing
☐ lots of switching around ☐ me somewhere in a pile
☐ other: _____

When I fantasize, I usually . . .

☐ think about one favorite fantasy for several weeks or months—
as long as it works for me
☐ fantasize several different scenarios about the same person
☐ switch to a new fantasy partner each time

I'm most likely to fantasize about . . .

☐ real experiences that I've enjoyed
☐ real experiences that I improve on
☐ completely made-up experiences

My fantasies . . .

☐ involve lots of buildup, seduction, or foreplay
☐ just cut to the chase

My fantasies include cuddling afterwards.

☐ true ☐ false

The idea of someone I know fantasizing about me is . . .

☐ sweet ☐ exciting ☐ creepy

The idea of being so alluring that people I know can't help but fantasize about me is . . .

☐ exciting ☐ uncomfortable

The biggest taboo I've broken in real life is:

_____

The biggest taboo I'd break only in fantasy is:

_____

The biggest taboo I'd actually like to break is:

_____

My fantasies usually involve . . .

☐ scenarios I'd like to explore in real life
☐ things that have already happened to me
☐ scenarios I enjoy thinking about, but wouldn't want to try
☐ a little of each

My fantasies usually involve . . .

☐ new partners ☐ new positions ☐ new locations
☐ all of the above

My fantasies usually involve . . .

☐ me acting differently ☐ other people treating me differently
☐ a little of each

My fantasies usually involve . . .

☐ more orgasms ☐ better orgasms
☐ more intimacy ☐ less intimacy
☐ exotic locations ☐ places I'm familiar with
☐ one partner ☐ multiple partners

The most important element in my fantasies is usually . . .

☐ the mood ☐ the setting ☐ the emotions involved
☐ my fantasy partner or partners ☐ the sex act involved

I'm most likely to fantasize about . . .

☐ characters from books ☐ characters from movies
☐ characters from television ☐ characters from mythology

My favorite characters that I've fantasized about are:

_____

I've noticed that they have this in common:

_____

_____

I'm most likely to incorporate a real person into my fantasy life when . . .

☐ he or she seems safe ☐ he or she seems dangerous
☐ he or she is attractive ☐ he or she is intelligent
☐ other: _____

The personality trait that my fantasy partners have in common is:

_____

_____

My fantasy partners tend to look like this:

_____

_____

My fantasy partners are more likely to be . . .

☐ warm and nurturing ☐ cold and forceful

☐ My fantasy partners need me more than I need them.
☐ I need my fantasy partners more than they need me.

☐ I choose my fantasy partners.
☐ My fantasy partners choose me.

☐ My fantasy partners are more likely to be overeager.
☐ My fantasy partners usually need to be seduced.

A fantasy in which I climax but my partner doesn't is . . .

☐ normal ☐ okay sometimes ☐ my favorite ☐ less exciting ☐ pointless

A fantasy in which my partner climaxes but I don't is . . .

☐ normal ☐ okay sometimes ☐ my favorite ☐ less exciting ☐ pointless

In my fantasies, I'm most likely to . . .

☐ climax right away ☐ hold out as long as possible

My fantasies usually . . .

☐ involve multiple orgasms ☐ build to one climactic orgasm

I sometimes wish my real-life partner would be . . .

☐ more experimental ☐ more tender
☐ more patient ☐ more forceful
☐ other: _____

I usually fantasize . . .

☐ in bed at night ☐ during the day, when I'm bored ☐ at work
☐ in the car/bus/train on my way to and from work
☐ whenever I see someone attractive

I usually fantasize . . .

☐ during sex ☐ while masturbating with my partner
☐ in addition to sex ☐ instead of sex

When I fantasize at home, I prefer to set the mood by . . .

☐ lighting candles ☐ playing music ☐ running a bath
☐ I don't bother setting a mood; I just get down to business
☐ other: _____

When I fantasize at home, I prefer to . . .

☐ undress completely ☐ wear sexy lingerie/underwear ☐ undress as I go

When I fantasize, I usually . . .

☐ masturbate ☐ keep it all in my mind

When I masturbate during a fantasy, I usually use . . .

☐ my hand ☐ a toy ☐ my partner

When I fantasize at home, I prefer to . . .

☐ get in the mood with a sexy movie
☐ get in the mood with erotic stories or a romance novel
☐ just use my imagination

In fantasies, I most enjoy the fact that . . .

☐ I get to behave differently ☐ others behave differently toward me

I've told my friends about my fantasies.

☐ yes ☐ no

I've talked to my partner about my fantasies.

☐ yes, all of them ☐ yes, some of them ☐ no, none at all

If a close friend were fantasizing about me, I'd want to know.

☐ yes ☐ no ☐ depends on the friend

If an acquaintance were fantasizing about me, I'd want to know.

☐ yes ☐ no ☐ depends on the acquaintance

If a colleague were fantasizing about me, I'd want to know.

☐ yes ☐ no ☐ depends on the person

I've told a friend that I've had fantasies about him or her.

☐ yes ☐ no
☐ I'd like to

I've told a colleague that I've had fantasies about him or her.

☐ yes ☐ no
☐ I'd like to

The idea of sharing my fantasies with my partner makes me feel . . .

☐ nervous ☐ excited ☐ What's the big deal?

I'm concerned about sharing my fantasies with my partner because . . .

- ☐ I'm worried my partner will be jealous
- ☐ I'm worried my partner will think I'm weird
- ☐ I'm worried that my partner will push me to try things with which I'm not comfortable
- ☐ none of these

Here's the closest my partner and I have come to actually fulfilling one of my fantasies:

_____

_____

_____

I'm hoping that sharing my fantasies with my partner will help us to explore more sexually.

- ☐ yes ☐ no

I'm hoping that sharing my fantasies with my partner will help build trust between us.

- ☐ yes ☐ no

I'm hoping that sharing my fantasies will help my partner share fantasies with me.

- ☐ yes ☐ no

Mostly I'm hoping that sharing my fantasies will turn my partner on.

- ☐ yes ☐ no
- ☐ you better believe it

Let's Role

chapter 2

Try This for Sighs

Costumes are . . .

     ☐ always fun ☐ too silly ☐ sometimes exciting ☐ essential

The idea of my partner showing up at my house dressed as a delivery boy is . . .

     ☐ always fun ☐ too silly ☐ sometimes exciting ☐ essential

The idea of dressing up with my partner as a French maid and her master is . . .

     ☐ always fun ☐ too silly ☐ sometimes exciting ☐ essential

The idea of dressing up with my partner as a valet and the lady of the house is . . .

     ☐ always fun ☐ too silly ☐ sometimes exciting ☐ essential

The idea of dressing up as a king and a scullery maid is . . .

     ☐ always fun ☐ too silly ☐ sometimes exciting ☐ essential

The idea of dressing up as a boss and a secretary is . . .

☐ always fun ☐ too silly ☐ sometimes exciting ☐ essential

The idea of dressing up as a doctor and a patient is . . .

☐ always fun ☐ too silly ☐ sometimes exciting ☐ essential

The idea of dressing up as a pirate and a captive is . . .

☐ always fun ☐ too silly ☐ sometimes exciting ☐ essential

The idea of dressing up as a schoolgirl and her professor is . . .

☐ always fun ☐ too silly ☐ sometimes exciting ☐ essential

The idea of dressing up as a schoolboy and his schoolmistress is . . .

☐ always fun ☐ too silly ☐ sometimes exciting ☐ essential

The idea of dressing up as a cowboy and a saloon girl is . . .

☐ always fun ☐ too silly ☐ sometimes exciting ☐ essential

The idea of dressing up as Tarzan and Jane is . . .

☐ always fun ☐ too silly ☐ sometimes exciting ☐ essential

The idea of dressing up as an athlete and a cheerleader is . . .

☐ always fun ☐ too silly ☐ sometimes exciting ☐ essential

The idea of dressing up as Venus and Apollo is . . .

☐ always fun ☐ too silly ☐ sometimes exciting ☐ essential

The idea of dressing up as President and an intern is . . .

☐ always fun ☐ too silly ☐ sometimes exciting ☐ essential

The idea of dressing up as a geisha and a samurai is . . .

☐ always fun ☐ too silly ☐ sometimes exciting ☐ essential

The idea of dressing up as a pimp and a hooker is . . .

☐ always fun ☐ too silly ☐ sometimes exciting ☐ essential

The idea of dressing up as a business traveler and a bar pickup is . . .

☐ always fun ☐ too silly ☐ sometimes exciting ☐ essential

The idea of dressing up as a sultan and his concubine is . . .

☐ always fun ☐ too silly ☐ sometimes exciting ☐ essential

The idea of dressing up as an Amazon queen and her captive is . . .

☐ always fun ☐ too silly ☐ sometimes exciting ☐ essential

The idea of dressing up as a master and a slave is . . .

☐ always fun ☐ too silly ☐ sometimes exciting ☐ essential

The idea of dressing up as Cinderella and Prince Charming is . . .

☐ always fun ☐ too silly ☐ sometimes exciting ☐ essential

The idea of dressing up as Caesar and Cleopatra is . . .

☐ always fun ☐ too silly ☐ sometimes exciting ☐ essential

The idea of dressing up as a vampire and a victim is . . .

☐ always fun ☐ too silly ☐ sometimes exciting ☐ essential

The idea of dressing up as a secret agent and an interrogator is . . .

☐ always fun ☐ too silly ☐ sometimes exciting ☐ essential

The idea of dressing up as a pilot and a flight attendant is . . .

☐ always fun ☐ too silly ☐ sometimes exciting ☐ essential

The idea of dressing up as a priest and a nun is . . .

☐ always fun ☐ too silly ☐ sometimes exciting ☐ essential

I'd like to incorporate role playing into my real-life sex.

☐ yes ☐ no ☐ I'm not sure.

Look at Me!

The idea of stripping for my partner is . . .

☐ hot ☐ warm ☐ not especially interesting ☐ out of the question

The idea of stripping in a club is . . .

☐ hot ☐ warm ☐ not especially interesting ☐ out of the question

The idea of stripping in a football stadium is . . .

☐ hot ☐ warm ☐ not especially interesting ☐ out of the question

The idea of stripping in a public park is . . .

☐ hot ☐ warm ☐ not especially interesting ☐ out of the question

The idea of being seen while masturbating is . . .

☐ ordinary ☐ exciting ☐ uncomfortable

The idea of being overheard while masturbating is . . .

☐ ordinary ☐ exciting ☐ uncomfortable

The idea of someone seeing or overhearing me masturbating and then coming in to join me is . . .

☐ ordinary ☐ exciting ☐ uncomfortable

The idea of seducing someone by allowing little glimpses of my body is . . .

☐ ordinary ☐ exciting ☐ uncomfortable

The idea of seducing someone by touching myself in front of them is . . .

☐ ordinary ☐ exciting ☐ uncomfortable

The idea of seducing someone by brushing up against them is . . .

☐ ordinary ☐ exciting ☐ uncomfortable

The idea of turning on a fantasy partner until he or she is unable to stop is . . .

☐ ordinary ☐ exciting ☐ uncomfortable

The idea of having sex somewhere we have to stay quiet is . . .

☐ hot ☐ warm ☐ not especially interesting ☐ out of the question

The idea of being as loud as I want is . . .

☐ hot ☐ warm ☐ not especially interesting ☐ out of the question

The idea of secretly watching my lover have sex with someone else is . . .

☐ a turn-on ☐ a turn-off ☐ I'm not sure

The idea of openly watching my lover have sex with someone else is . . .

☐ a turn-on ☐ a turn-off ☐ I'm not sure

The idea of my lover secretly watching me have sex with someone else is . . .

☐ a turn-on ☐ a turn-off ☐ I'm not sure

The idea of my lover openly watching me have sex with someone else is . . .

☐ a turn-on ☐ a turn-off ☐ I'm not sure

The idea of making my partner so aroused that he or she can't hide it in public is . . .

☐ ordinary ☐ exciting ☐ uncomfortable

The idea of making a friend so aroused that he or she can't hide it in public is . . .

☐ ordinary ☐ exciting ☐ uncomfortable

The idea of making a colleague so aroused that he or she can't hide it in public is . . .

☐ ordinary ☐ exciting ☐ uncomfortable

The idea of making a stranger so aroused that he or she can't hide it in public is . . .

☐ ordinary ☐ exciting ☐ uncomfortable

The idea of walking down the street in revealing clothes is . . .

☐ ordinary ☐ exciting ☐ uncomfortable

The idea of walking down the street naked is . . .

☐ ordinary ☐ exciting ☐ uncomfortable

The idea of returning to a party after I've obviously had sex is . . .

☐ ordinary ☐ exciting ☐ uncomfortable

The idea of going to work after I've obviously had sex is . . .

☐ ordinary ☐ exciting ☐ uncomfortable

The idea of going to church after I've obviously had sex is . . .

☐ ordinary ☐ exciting ☐ uncomfortable

I'd like to try having sex in real life in a place where I might get caught.

☐ yes ☐ no ☐ I don't know

I'd like to try exhibitionism in real life.

☐ yes ☐ no ☐ I don't know

I'd like to try voyeurism in real life.

☐ yes ☐ no ☐ I don't know

The idea of overhearing someone masturbate is . . .

☐ ordinary ☐ exciting ☐ uncomfortable

The idea of overhearing someone else have sex is . . .

☐ ordinary ☐ exciting ☐ uncomfortable

The idea of secretly watching someone masturbate is . . .

☐ ordinary ☐ exciting ☐ uncomfortable

The idea of secretly watching someone have sex is . . .

☐ ordinary ☐ exciting ☐ uncomfortable

The idea of openly watching someone masturbate is . . .

☐ ordinary ☐ exciting ☐ uncomfortable

The idea of openly watching someone have sex is . . .

☐ ordinary ☐ exciting ☐ uncomfortable

The idea of videotaping myself having sex is . . .

☐ ordinary ☐ exciting ☐ uncomfortable

I would want to videotape myself having sex in real life.

☐ yes ☐ no ☐ I don't know

Special Friends

chapter 3

The More, the Merrier

Inviting a woman to join me and my partner sounds . . .

    ☐ old hat ☐ perfect ☐ intriguing
    ☐ like something that's fun to think about, but not try ☐ awful

Inviting a man to join us sounds . . .

    ☐ old hat ☐ perfect ☐ intriguing
    ☐ like something that's fun to think about, but not try ☐ awful

Inviting another couple to join us sounds . . .

    ☐ old hat ☐ perfect ☐ intriguing
    ☐ like something that's fun to think about, but not try ☐ awful

The idea of taking part in an orgy or swingers' party sounds . . .

    ☐ old hat ☐ perfect ☐ intriguing
    ☐ like something that's fun to think about, but not try ☐ awful

If someone were to join us, I'd prefer if that person (or people) were . . .

    ☐ someone me and my partner picked out together
    ☐ someone my partner has picked
    ☐ someone I've picked

If someone were to join us, I'd prefer if that person (or people) were . . .

☐ a trusted friend ☐ an acquaintance ☐ a total stranger ☐ paid

I'd like to actually invite someone to join me and my partner.

☐ yes ☐ no ☐ I'm not sure

If my partner and I actually had someone join us, I'd be worried that . . .

☐ I'd be jealous ☐ my partner would be jealous ☐ both

Other concerns would be . . .

☐ sexually transmitted diseases
☐ I just wouldn't enjoy it
☐ my partner just wouldn't enjoy it
☐ our new playmate might tell someone about it
☐ my partner would only want to have someone join us once
☐ my partner would always want to have someone join us
☐ other: _____

If someone were to join me and my partner, I'd be . . .

☐ more focused on our new playmate
☐ more focused on my experience
☐ more focused on my partner's reactions

I've already got a potential playmate in mind.

☐ true ☐ false

I think my partner already has a potential playmate in mind.

☐ true ☐ false

Inviting someone to join me and my partner so I can experiment with a gender outside my usual preference sounds . . .

☐ safer ☐ less safe

If we were to really have someone join us, I'd be doing it . . .

☐ more for me ☐ more for my partner ☐ for both of us

A Walk on the Wild Side

The idea of having sex with someone outside my usual gender preference is . . .
- ☐ intriguing
- ☐ definitely a turn-on
- ☐ a turn-on in theory, but not something I'd do
- ☐ definitely a turn-off
- ☐ impossible: I'm bisexual

The appeal of having sex with a woman is . . .
- ☐ exploring a woman's body
- ☐ the idea that a woman might be more tender
- ☐ other: _____

The appeal of having sex with a man is . . .
- ☐ exploring a man's body
- ☐ the idea that a man might be stronger
- ☐ other: _____

In my fantasy about someone outside my gender preference, I'd want my fantasy partner to teach me what to do.
- ☐ true ☐ false

It's hotter to think about seducing someone outside my usual gender preference.
- ☐ true ☐ false

It's hotter to think about someone outside my usual gender preference seducing me.
- ☐ true ☐ false

I fantasize more often about . . .
- ☐ starting an ongoing relationship with someone outside my usual gender preference
- ☐ sleeping with someone outside my usual gender preference just once

In real life, I'd be more interested in . . .

- [ ] starting an ongoing relationship with someone outside my usual gender preference
- [ ] sleeping with someone outside my usual gender preference just once

My fantasy partner outside my usual gender preference is usually . . .

- [ ] a close friend
- [ ] a work colleague
- [ ] an acquaintance or someone I've noticed in real life
- [ ] a complete stranger

My fantasy partner outside my usual gender preference is usually . . .

- [ ] a teacher, work supervisor, or other authority figure
- [ ] a subordinate [ ] an equal

In my fantasy, my tryst with someone outside my usual gender preference is . . .

- [ ] a secret [ ] something my partner knows about and approves of
- [ ] something that shocks my partner [ ] public

I'd like to try having sex with someone outside my usual gender preference in real life.

- [ ] yes [ ] no [ ] I'm not sure [ ] I already have

I'd try having sex with someone outside my usual gender preference if . . .

- [ ] I knew it would be kept a secret
- [ ] my partner knew and approved
- [ ] my partner could be there and watch
- [ ] I already have

The thing that's stopping me from exploring with someone outside my usual gender preference is . . .

- [ ] my commitment to my partner
- [ ] concerns about what that would mean about my sexual identity
- [ ] concerns about friends, family, or community disapproval if someone found out
- [ ] I just don't think I'd like it.

Exchanging More Than Glances

The idea of sleeping with a stranger I've never met before is . . .
   ☐ exciting ☐ interesting ☐ uncomfortable

The idea of picking up a stranger in a local bar is . . .
   ☐ exciting ☐ creepy

The idea of sleeping with a stranger in a foreign country is . . .
   ☐ exciting ☐ creepy

The idea of sleeping with a stranger and never learning his or her name is . . .
   ☐ exciting ☐ creepy

The idea of sleeping with a stranger on a cross-country plane or train trip is . . .
   ☐ exciting ☐ creepy

The idea of sleeping with a masked stranger is . . .
   ☐ exciting ☐ creepy

The idea of sleeping with a stranger I can't see at all is . . .
   ☐ exciting ☐ creepy

What turns me on about a stranger fantasy is choosing and seducing the stranger.
   ☐ true ☐ false

What turns me on about a stranger fantasy is the stranger choosing and seducing me.
   ☐ true ☐ false

What turns me on about a stranger fantasy is starting a completely new relationship.

   ☐ true ☐ false

What turns me on about a stranger fantasy is the complete lack of strings attached.

   ☐ true ☐ false

What turns me on about a stranger fantasy is the idea of exploring a completely new body.

   ☐ true ☐ false

What turns me on about a stranger fantasy is the idea of being able to turn someone on so much that he or she can't resist.

   ☐ true ☐ false

What turns me on about a stranger fantasy is the complete lack of consequences.

   ☐ true ☐ false

What turns me on about a stranger fantasy is the ability to create a new persona for myself.

   ☐ true ☐ false

What turns me on about a stranger fantasy is the ability to demand whatever I want without inhibitions.

   ☐ true ☐ false

What turns me on about a stranger fantasy is diving right in and getting on with it.

   ☐ true ☐ false

I'd actually want to role-play picking up my partner as a stranger.

   ☐ yes ☐ no

I've actually slept with a stranger in real life.

☐ true ☐ false

I enjoyed the experience.

☐ yes ☐ no ☐ I told you, I haven't done it.

A Little Game of "Who Would You Do?"

I Prefer Men:

☐ Matthew McConaughey or ☐ Leonardo DiCaprio

☐ The Wolf Man or ☐ Dracula

☐ Luke Skywalker or ☐ Han Solo

☐ Zach Braff or ☐ Donald Faison

☐ Bill Paxton or ☐ Bill Pullman

☐ Cary Grant or ☐ Clark Gable

☐ Arnold Schwarzenegger or ☐ Sylvester Stallone

☐ Taye Diggs or ☐ Denzel Washington

☐ Jet Li or ☐ Chow Yun-Fat

☐ Fred MacMurray or ☐ Robert Young

☐ Heathcliff Huxtable or ☐ Tim Taylor

☐ John Cusack or ☐ Jeremy Piven

☐ Christopher Meloni or ☐ Chris Noth

☐ Bill Clinton or ☐ Al Gore

☐ Bill Clinton or ☐ George W. Bush

☐ Tom Selleck in *Magnum, P.I.* or ☐ Tom Selleck in *Friends*

☐ Daniel Dae Kim or ☐ Josh Holloway

☐ George Clooney or ☐ Brad Pitt

☐ Heath Ledger or ☐ Jake Gyllenhaal

☐ Christian Slater or ☐ Christian Bale

☐ Prince William or ☐ Prince Harry

☐ Homer Simpson or ☐ Hank Hill

☐ Legolas or ☐ Aragorn

☐ Heathcliff from *Wuthering Heights* or ☐ Mr. Rochester from *Jane Eyre*

☐ Paul Rudd or ☐ Steve Carell

☐ Shia LaBeouf or ☐ Justin Long

☐ Superman or ☐ Batman

☐ Matt Damon or ☐ Ben Affleck

☐ Ryan Phillipe or ☐ Matt Dillon

☐ Jon Stewart or ☐ Stephen Colbert

☐ Mario Lopez or ☐ Mark-Paul Gosselaar

☐ Bob Dylan or ☐ Lou Reed

☐ Mark McGrath or ☐ Dave Grohl

☐ Metallica or ☐ Spinal Tap

☐ Mr. Darcy from *Pride and Prejudice* or ☐ Mr. Knightley from *Emma*

☐ Hugh Jackman or ☐ Hugh Grant

☐ Steve Martin or ☐ Bill Murray

☐ Mick Jagger or ☐ Keith Richards

☐ Bono or ☐ The Edge

☐ Sting or ☐ David Bowie

☐ Benicio Del Toro or ☐ John Leguizamo

☐ Ashton Kutcher or ☐ Bruce Willis

☐ Will Ferrell or ☐ Ben Stiller

☐ Luke Wilson or ☐ Owen Wilson

☐ George Washington or ☐ Thomas Jefferson

☐ Abraham Lincoln or ☐ Ulysses S. Grant

☐ Johnny Depp or ☐ Orlando Bloom

☐ Michael Showalter or ☐ Michael Ian Black

☐ Steve Buscemi or ☐ Billy Bob Thornton

☐ Luke Perry or ☐ Jason Priestley

☐ Eddie Izzard or ☐ Denis Leary

☐ Justin Timberlake or ☐ John Mayer

☐ Usher or ☐ Kanye West

☐ Ryan Seacrest or ☐ Simon Cowell

☐ Ice Cube or ☐ Ice T

☐ Robert De Niro or ☐ Harvey Keitel

☐ Borat or ☐ Ali G

☐ Tom Waits or ☐ Beck

☐ Sean Connery or ☐ Daniel Craig

☐ Colin Firth or ☐ Colin Farrell

I Prefer Women:

☐ Salma Hayek or ☐ Penélope Cruz

☐ Jessica Alba or ☐ Jennifer Garner

☐ Eva Longoria or ☐ Teri Hatcher

☐ Angelina Jolie or ☐ Jennifer Aniston

☐ Scarlett Johansson or ☐ Claire Danes

☐ Xena or ☐ Gabrielle

☐ Heather Locklear or ☐ Denise Richards

☐ Beyoncé or ☐ Shakira

☐ Carmen Electra or ☐ Pamela Anderson

☐ Alyssa Milano or ☐ Jessica Biel

☐ Lucille Ball or ☐ Carol Burnett

☐ Jennifer Lopez or ☐ Catherine Zeta-Jones

☐ Paris or ☐ Nicole

☐ Jaime Pressly or ☐ Nadine Velazquez

☐ Halle Berry or ☐ Jada Pinkett Smith

☐ Jessica Simpson or ☐ Ashlee Simpson

☐ Julie Newmar or ☐ Eartha Kitt

☐ Greta Garbo or ☐ Marlene Dietrich

☐ Bettie Page or ☐ Lana Turner

☐ Jessica Rabbit or ☐ Betty Boop

☐ Mandy Moore or ☐ Hilary Duff

- Cleopatra or ☐ Elizabeth I
- Gabrielle Reece or ☐ Mia Hamm
- Rogue or ☐ Storm
- Wonder Woman or ☐ The Bionic Woman
- Naomi Watts or ☐ Nicole Kidman
- Tyra Banks or ☐ Naomi Campbell
- Cindy Crawford or ☐ Elizabeth Hurley
- Melissa Etheridge or ☐ Joan Jett
- Cat Power or ☐ Liz Phair
- Katie Couric or ☐ Diane Sawyer
- Tina Fey or ☐ Amy Poehler
- Molly Ringwald or ☐ Ally Sheedy
- Lili Taylor or ☐ Fairuza Balk
- Sarah Silverman or ☐ Janeane Garofalo
- America Ferrera or ☐ Ana Ortiz
- Tonya Harding or ☐ Nancy Kerrigan
- Rachel Bilson or ☐ Mischa Barton
- The Spice Girls or ☐ The Pussycat Dolls
- Marge Simpson or ☐ Lois Griffin
- Aphrodite or ☐ Helen of Troy
- Madame Bovary or ☐ Lady Chatterley
- Annie Oakley or ☐ Calamity Jane
- Yasmine Bleeth or ☐ Alexandra Paul
- Drew Barrymore or ☐ Cameron Diaz
- Sarah Jessica Parker or ☐ Kim Cattrall
- Glinda the Good Witch or ☐ The Wicked Witch of the West
- Princess Leia or ☐ Queen Amidala
- Jennifer Beals or ☐ Leisha Hailey
- Katharine Hepburn or ☐ Audrey Hepburn

☐ Arwen or ☐ Galadriel

☐ PJ Harvey or ☐ Chrissie Hynde

☐ Neve Campbell or ☐ Jennifer Love Hewitt

☐ Mena Suvari or ☐ Thora Birch

☐ Gisele Bündchen or ☐ Heidi Klum

☐ Linda Evangelista or ☐ Christy Turlington

☐ Heather Graham or ☐ Kate Hudson

☐ Faith Hill or ☐ Shania Twain

☐ Katee Sackhoff or ☐ Tricia Helfer

☐ Hillary Clinton or ☐ Condoleezza Rice

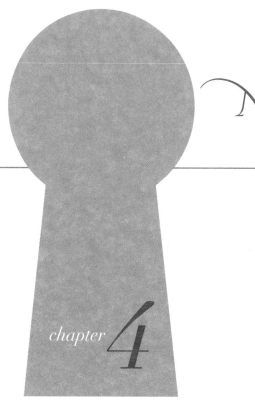

Not-So-Secret Fantasies

chapter 4

How Well Do You Know Your Partner?

I feel like I have a pretty good idea of what my partner's fantasies are.

- [ ] yes, because we've talked about them
- [ ] yes, because I think I can make a pretty good guess
- [ ] no, we have never discussed them

My partner fantasizes more about . . .

- [ ] me [ ] past lovers [ ] celebrities [ ] attractive strangers
- [ ] friends or acquaintances

My partner fantasizes about sex that is . . .

- [ ] rougher than we have [ ] gentler than we have [ ] about the same

My partner fantasizes about sex that is . . .

- [ ] kinkier than we have [ ] more "vanilla" than we have
- [ ] about the same

My partner fantasizes about . . .

- [ ] more foreplay than we have [ ] less foreplay than we have

My partner fantasizes about . . .

    ☐ more intimacy ☐ more physicality

Here's how I think my partner's fantasy objects might be different than
I am physically:

_____

Here's how the personalities of my partner's fantasy objects might be
different than mine:

_____

If I walked in on my partner fantasizing and masturbating I'd feel . . .

    ☐ threatened ☐ embarrassed ☐ turned on
    ☐ curious ☐ what's the big deal?

If I walked in on my partner fantasizing and masturbating I'd most likely . . .

    ☐ apologize for not knocking and leave ☐ join in
    ☐ get upset ☐ ask my partner about the fantasy

I think masturbation is . . .

    ☐ healthy ☐ only for people who aren't already having sex
    ☐ something I'm not quite comfortable with

I'd feel comfortable making up a fantasy to tell my partner while he or she
masturbated.

    ☐ true ☐ false

I'd feel comfortable talking with my partner about his or her fantasies.

    ☐ true ☐ false

I think learning about my partner's fantasies would be good for our sex life.

    ☐ true ☐ false

I'd be concerned about hearing my partner's fantasies because . . .

    ☐ I'd be jealous
    ☐ I'd be nervous about living up to them
    ☐ I don't want to encourage my partner to think about something I'm
    not comfortable with
    ☐ other: _____

If I found out my partner fantasizes about something that's a turnoff
for me, I'd . . .

    ☐ let it go, as long as it stays a fantasy
    ☐ try to see the appeal
    ☐ break up
    ☐ it depends on the fantasy
    ☐ other: _____

Something I think my partner fantasizes about that I'd like to do:

_____

_____

Something I think my partner fantasizes about that I'd rather not do:

_____

_____

The taboo I think my partner most fantasizes about breaking is:

_____

I'd be comfortable fulfilling a fantasy that involved me giving but not
receiving pleasure.

    ☐ yes ☐ no

I'd be comfortable fulfilling a fantasy that involved my partner giving but
not receiving pleasure.

    ☐ yes ☐ no

I think my partner's fantasy is . . .

☐ elaborate, including a detailed storyline ☐ simply sex

I think my partner's fantasy . . .

☐ is a quickie ☐ lasts all night

My partner's fantasy persona is:

_____

I think my partner's favorite fantasy position is:

_____

I think my partner's fantasies draw most from . . .

☐ books ☐ mainstream movies ☐ porn movies
☐ magazines ☐ comics
☐ other: _____

In real life, my partner prefers to be . . .

☐ dominant ☐ submissive ☐ a little of each

In fantasy, my partner prefers to be . . .

☐ dominant ☐ submissive ☐ a little of each

In real life, my partner prefers to be . . .

☐ pursued ☐ the pursuer

In fantasy, my partner prefers to be . . .

☐ pursued ☐ the pursuer

Here's how I think my partner behaves differently overall in his or her fantasies:

_____

_____

My partner's ideal fantasy job would be:

_____

My partner's ideal fantasy time period would be:

_____

My partner's ideal fantasy setting would be:

_____

My partner's ideal fantasy plot would be:

_____

_____

_____

If my partner were to fantasize about someone joining us, I'm pretty sure that person would be:

_____

If the opportunity came up, I'd really like that person to join us.

☐ yes ☐ no ☐ hell, yes! ☐ hell, no!

Why?

_____

Here's how I think my partner's fantasies are like mine:

_____

Here's how I think my partner's fantasies are different from mine:

_____

Here's how I'd like to appear in my partner's fantasies:

_____

Here's how I think I actually appear in my partner's fantasies:

_____

Here's how I'd like to behave in my partner's fantasies:

_____

_____

_____

Here's how I think I actually behave in my partner's fantasies:

_____

_____

Here's what I think I'm usually wearing in my partner's fantasies:

_____

_____

Based on what I know, I think my partner's ideal fantasy would be this:

_____

_____

_____

_____

_____

Here's the closest thing to that fantasy that I'd actually be willing to try:

_____

_____

_____

_____

_____

Based on what I know, I think a fantasy that would turn both of us on would be this:

_____

_____

_____

Here's the closest thing to that fantasy that I'd actually be willing to try:

_____

_____

_____

Hey, partner! How'd I do?

_____

_____

_____

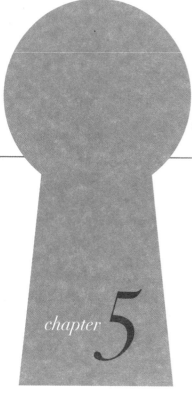

Reality, Tweaked

chapter 5

PERFECTION IS A STATE OF MIND

Imagine a perfect night with your partner, with money as no object. He or she tends to your every desire, exactly as you would like.

What is the setting?

_____

_____

What, if anything, do you eat?

_____

What are the sounds?

_____

What are the scents?

_____

What are you wearing?

_____

What is your partner wearing?

_____

What happens?

_____

_____

What position or positions do you use?

_____

How does your partner behave?

_____

How is your partner different from how he or she usually is?

_____

How do you behave?

_____

How do you feel?

_____

How are you different from who you are in real life?

_____

Which parts of this fantasy do you feel you can make happen?

_____

Which parts do you think will never happen?

_____

Why?

_____

_____

Will you be putting this fantasy on your list of things to actually try?

☐ yes ☐ no

I'd like my partner to do this all or most of the time:

_____

I'd like my partner to do this some, but not all, of the time:

_____

I'd like my partner to do this just once:

_____

MORE THAN THE SUM OF YOUR PARTS

You've created the perfect partner and the perfect evening. Now, create the perfect you . . .

I have fantasized about changes to my body.

☐ true ☐ false

When I fantasize about changing my body, I fantasize about being . . .

☐ more athletic ☐ more voluptuous ☐ more slender
☐ taller ☐ shorter

I have fantasized about being . . .

☐ a blonde ☐ a brunette ☐ a redhead
☐ dyed with blue/green/purple/whatever I want

My fantasy hair is . . .

☐ longer ☐ shorter ☐ curlier ☐ straighter ☐ fuller ☐ wilder
☐ a Mohawk ☐ gone

My eyes in my fantasies are . . .

☐ brown ☐ hazel ☐ green ☐ blue ☐ gray ☐ violet

My legs in my fantasies are . . .

☐ longer ☐ shorter ☐ stronger ☐ more slender
☐ more voluptuous

I have fantasized about having . . .

☐ bigger breasts ☐ smaller breasts ☐ I like mine how they are

I've fantasized about changing my . . .

☐ arms ☐ hands ☐ feet ☐ neck ☐ other:

_____

I have fantasized about being another race.

☐ true ☐ false

I have fantasized about having a completely different body or being a
completely different person.

☐ true ☐ false

I have fantasized about being a celebrity.

☐ true ☐ false

I have fantasized about being a mythical being.

☐ true ☐ false

This is the way my favorite "fantasy me" looks, from head to toe:

_____

_____

Looking like this is appealing because:

_____

_____

I have fantasized about being a man.

☐ true ☐ false

I have fantasized about being a woman.

☐ true ☐ false

When I fantasize about being a man, my partners are . . .

☐ men ☐ women ☐ anyone is fair game

When I fantasize about being a woman, my partners are . . .

☐ men ☐ women ☐ anyone is fair game

The appeal of being a man in a fantasy is . . .

☐ the power
☐ trying out the new equipment
☐ getting to behave differently/more aggressively
☐ nonexistent
☐ other: _____

The appeal of being a woman in a fantasy is . . .

☐ the power
☐ trying out the new equipment
☐ getting to behave differently/more aggressively
☐ nonexistent
☐ other: _____

Fantasy Accessories

chapter **6**

Accessories That You Play

Given the choice, I'd prefer . . .
- ☐ a sexy mainstream movie
- ☐ a sexy book
- ☐ a "nude" magazine

I'd most enjoy . . .
- ☐ using an erotic movie to get us in the mood
- ☐ having an erotic movie playing while we're having sex
- ☐ being in the erotic movie

I find pornography to be . . .
- ☐ too graphic
- ☐ a good way to get ideas
- ☐ a spicy addition to real-life sex
- ☐ in general, a turn-on
- ☐ in general, a turn-off
- ☐ it depends on the movie and my mood

I get ideas about possible fantasy plots from pornography.
- ☐ true ☐ false

I get ideas about possible fantasy positions from porn.

☐ true ☐ false

I get ideas about my fantasy partners from porn.

☐ true ☐ false

I'd like to actually reproduce a scene from a porn flick.

☐ true ☐ false

I'm more likely to fantasize about . . .

☐ something I've seen in a porn video
☐ something I've seen in a mainstream movie
☐ something I've read

I fantasize about looking like a porn star.

☐ true ☐ false
☐ I already do look like one

I'd like to actually be a porn star.

☐ true ☐ false
☐ I already am a porn star

Given the choice, I'd prefer to watch . . .

☐ a mainstream movie with erotic elements
☐ a straight-up porn flick

I'd rather watch pornography . . .

☐ alone ☐ with my partner ☐ not at all

Having a porn movie on during sex is . . .

☐ essential
☐ a way to add spice sometimes
☐ distracting
☐ gross

I'm concerned about watching porn with my partner because . . .

- ☐ I haven't seen it before and I think I won't like it
- ☐ I'm worried my partner will like the actors' bodies more than mine
- ☐ I'm worried that my partner will want to try things in the movie that I'm not comfortable with
- ☐ I'm worried that my partner won't like it
- ☐ I just don't like porn

I'd be interested in watching porn with my partner if . . .

- ☐ I knew it would be arousing for both of us
- ☐ I knew it would be arousing for at least one of us
- ☐ I thought it would give us some new ideas
- ☐ the movies were better made

Here's what I like about pornography:

_____

_____

Here's what I don't like:

_____

_____

Here's how I think porn influences my partner's fantasies:

_____

_____

_____

Here's how porn influences my fantasies:

_____

_____

_____

Here's how I'd change the plots of porn movies to make them more like my fantasies:

_____

_____

Here's how I'd change the actors in porn movies:

_____

_____

Here's how I'd change the way the characters relate to each other:

_____

_____

Here's how I'd change the sex itself:

_____

_____

If I were to write, direct, cast, and star in my own personal porn film, here's
how it would go:

_____

_____

_____

. . . and here's who would get to see it:

_____

Accessories That You Play with

The idea of experimenting with sex toys is . . .
 ☐ ordinary ☐ exciting ☐ uncomfortable

The idea of being penetrated with a toy is . . .
 ☐ ordinary ☐ exciting ☐ uncomfortable

The idea of penetrating my partner with a sex toy is . . .
 ☐ ordinary ☐ exciting ☐ uncomfortable

Sex toys should . . .

- ☐ look silly and fun, because they are
- ☐ look like they mean business
- ☐ not be anywhere near my fantasies

Vibrators have a place in my real life.

☐ yes ☐ no

Vibrators have a place in my fantasy life.

☐ yes ☐ no

When it comes to vibrators, I prefer to be on . . .

☐ the giving end ☐ the receiving end

Dildos have a place in my real life.

☐ yes ☐ no

Dildos have a place in my fantasy life.

☐ yes ☐ no

When it comes to dildos, I prefer to be on . . .

☐ the giving end ☐ the receiving end

I've fantasized about being handcuffed during sex.

☐ yes ☐ no

I've fantasized about doing the cuffing.

☐ yes ☐ no

I play with handcuffs in real life.

☐ yes ☐ no ☐ I'd like to

I've fantasized about using more complicated restraints, like leather straps.

☐ yes ☐ no

I've fantasized about being the one restrained.

☐ yes ☐ no

I've played with restraints in real life.

☐ yes ☐ no ☐ I'd like to

I've fantasized about being blindfolded during sex.

☐ yes ☐ no

I've fantasized about doing the blindfolding.

☐ yes ☐ no

I play with blindfolds in real life.

☐ yes ☐ no ☐ I'd like to

I've fantasized about using a swing during sex.

☐ yes ☐ no

I've played on a swing during sex in real life.

☐ yes ☐ no ☐ I'd like to

I've fantasized about using ice during sex.

☐ yes ☐ no

I've fantasized about having ice used on me.

☐ yes ☐ no

I've played with ice during sex in real life.

☐ yes ☐ no ☐ I'd like to

I've fantasized about giving a massage with scented oils or lubricants.

☐ yes ☐ no

I've fantasized about getting a massage with scented oils or lubricants.

☐ yes ☐ no

I've used scented oils or lubricants in real life.

☐ yes ☐ no ☐ I'd like to

I've fantasized about covering my partner in whipped cream.

☐ yes ☐ no

I've fantasized about being covered in whipped cream.

☐ yes ☐ no

I've played with whipped cream during sex in real life.

☐ yes ☐ no ☐ I'd like to

I've fantasized about giving my partner a massage with fur mittens.

☐ yes ☐ no

I've fantasized about getting a massage with fur mittens.

☐ yes ☐ no

I've played with fur during sex in real life.

☐ yes ☐ no ☐ I'd like to

I've fantasized about having hot wax dripped on me.

☐ yes ☐ no

I've fantasized about doing the dripping.

☐ yes ☐ no

I've played with hot wax during sex in real life.

☐ yes ☐ no ☐ I'd like to

I've fantasized about being tickled with feathers.

☐ yes ☐ no

I've fantasized about doing the tickling.

☐ yes ☐ no

I've played with feathers during sex in real life.

☐ yes ☐ no ☐ I'd like to

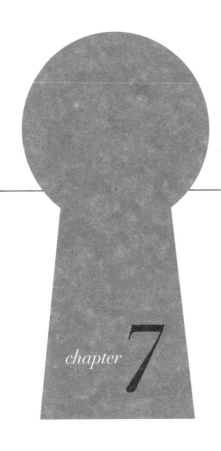

Power Games

chapter *7*

The Edge of Pleasure

The thought of seducing someone who isn't interesting to me at first is . . .
☐ ordinary ☐ exciting ☐ uncomfortable

The idea of seducing a virgin is . . .
☐ ordinary ☐ exciting ☐ uncomfortable

The thought of seducing someone much older than me is . . .
☐ ordinary ☐ exciting ☐ uncomfortable

The thought of seducing someone much younger than me (but still legal) is . . .
☐ ordinary ☐ exciting ☐ uncomfortable

The thought of seducing someone who has never slept with someone of my gender before is . . .
☐ ordinary ☐ exciting ☐ uncomfortable

When I have sex in real life . . .
☐ I need to know that I'm always safe
☐ I like things to be a little bit dangerous

In my fantasies . . .

- [ ] I'm always safe
- [ ] I live a little bit on the edge
- [ ] I'm not safe at all

The idea of giving up control in a fantasy sounds . . .

- [ ] exciting [ ] like a relief [ ] scary [ ] like the usual

The idea of taking total control in a fantasy sounds . . .

- [ ] exciting [ ] like a relief [ ] scary [ ] like the usual

The idea of having my wrists pinned or held over my head during sex is . . .

- [ ] exciting [ ] scary [ ] both exciting and scary [ ] a turn-off

The idea of having my wrists tied or handcuffed during sex is . . .

- [ ] exciting [ ] scary [ ] both exciting and scary [ ] a turn-off

The idea of having my wrists and ankles tied during sex is . . .

- [ ] exciting [ ] scary [ ] both exciting and scary [ ] a turn-off

I'd prefer . . .

- [ ] silk scarves
- [ ] ropes
- [ ] fuzzy handcuffs
- [ ] real handcuffs
- [ ] leather
- [ ] no restraints, please!

The idea of having my mouth covered or gagged during sex is . . .

- [ ] exciting [ ] scary [ ] both exciting and scary [ ] a turn-off

The idea of tying up my partner during sex is . . .

- [ ] exciting [ ] scary [ ] both exciting and scary [ ] a turn-off

The idea of tying a gag around my partner's mouth during sex is . . .

☐ exciting ☐ scary ☐ both exciting and scary ☐ a turn-off

The idea of BDSM (bondage & discipline/dominance & submission/sadism & masochism) activities being a part of sex is . . .

☐ out of the question
☐ okay, as long as it's mild
☐ what I've been waiting for

The idea of pain being a part of sex is . . .

☐ a turn-on ☐ a turn-off ☐ neither here nor there

The idea of giving or receiving more intense pain during sex is . . .

☐ a turn-on ☐ a turn-off ☐ neither here nor there

If BDSM were a part of sex, I would prefer to . . .

☐ dominate ☐ submit ☐ try out a little of each

The idea of comforting my fantasy partner after I've been the dominant and he or she has been the submissive is . . .

☐ a turn-on ☐ a turn-off ☐ neither here nor there

The idea of being comforted by my fantasy partner after I've been the submissive and he or she has been the dominant is . . .

☐ a turn-on ☐ a turn-off ☐ neither here nor there

The idea of being spanked is . . .

☐ a turn-on ☐ a turn-off ☐ neither here nor there

The idea of spanking my partner is . . .

☐ a turn-on ☐ a turn-off ☐ neither here nor there

The idea of being slapped is . . .

☐ a turn-on ☐ a turn-off ☐ neither here nor there

The idea of slapping my partner is . . .

☐ a turn-on ☐ a turn-off ☐ neither here nor there

The idea of being flogged is . . .

☐ a turn-on ☐ a turn-off ☐ neither here nor there

The idea of flogging my partner is . . .

☐ a turn-on ☐ a turn-off ☐ neither here nor there

I'd enjoy making my fantasy partner do small tasks, like massaging my shoulders or getting me a drink.

☐ true ☐ false

I'd enjoy making my fantasy partner tend to all of my sexual needs.

☐ true ☐ false

The idea of making my fantasy partner beg me for sex is . . .

☐ a turn-on ☐ a turn-off ☐ neither here nor there

I'd enjoy making my fantasy partner crawl for me.

☐ true ☐ false

I'd enjoy making my fantasy partner lick or kiss my shoes.

☐ true ☐ false

The idea of physical or verbal humiliation being a part of sex is . . .

☐ a turn-on ☐ a turn-off ☐ neither here nor there

If humiliation were a part of sex, I'd want to . . .

☐ be humiliated ☐ do the humiliating ☐ try out a little of each

If I had to choose just one, I'd . . .

☐ only give pleasure ☐ only receive pleasure

I'd be interested in including dominance and submission in my real-life sex.

☐ not at all ☐ occasionally ☐ most of the time ☐ all the time

I'd be interested in including bondage in my real-life sex.

☐ not at all ☐ occasionally ☐ most of the time ☐ all the time

I'd be interested in including sadomasochism in my real-life sex.

☐ not at all ☐ occasionally ☐ most of the time ☐ all the time

The Thrill of Danger

chapter 8

Planes, Trains, and Automobiles

The idea of just heavy petting, high-school style, in a car is . . .
☐ hot ☐ warm ☐ not especially interesting ☐ out of the question

The idea of having sex on a Ferris wheel is . . .
☐ hot ☐ warm ☐ not especially interesting ☐ out of the question

The idea of having sex on a speedboat is . . .
☐ hot ☐ warm ☐ not especially interesting ☐ out of the question

The idea of having sex on a luxury yacht is . . .
☐ hot ☐ warm ☐ not especially interesting ☐ out of the question

The idea of having sex in the back of a taxi is . . .
☐ hot ☐ warm ☐ not especially interesting ☐ out of the question

The idea of giving my partner a hand job while he or she is driving is . . .
☐ hot ☐ warm ☐ not especially interesting ☐ out of the question

The idea of giving my partner oral sex while he or she is driving is . . .

☐ hot ☐ warm ☐ not especially interesting ☐ out of the question

The idea of being manually pleasured while driving is . . .

☐ hot ☐ warm ☐ not especially interesting ☐ out of the question

The idea of receiving oral sex while driving is . . .

☐ hot ☐ warm ☐ not especially interesting ☐ out of the question

The idea of sex in the backseat of a car while someone else is driving is . . .

☐ hot ☐ warm ☐ not especially interesting ☐ out of the question

The idea of sex in a rowboat on a peaceful lake is . . .

☐ hot ☐ warm ☐ not especially interesting ☐ out of the question

The idea of sex on a carnival ride like the Tunnel of Love is . . .

☐ hot ☐ warm ☐ not especially interesting ☐ out of the question

The idea of having sex on a cross-country train is . . .

☐ hot ☐ warm ☐ not especially interesting ☐ out of the question

The idea of having sex on the subway is . . .

☐ hot ☐ warm ☐ not especially interesting ☐ out of the question

The idea of having sex in an airplane restroom is . . .

☐ hot ☐ warm ☐ not especially interesting ☐ out of the question

The idea of having sex in the middle of first class on an airplane is . . .

☐ hot ☐ warm ☐ not especially interesting ☐ out of the question

The idea of having sex in a small, two-person plane is . . .

☐ hot ☐ warm ☐ not especially interesting ☐ out of the question

The idea of sex on a private jet is . . .

⬜ hot ⬜ warm ⬜ not especially interesting ⬜ out of the question

The idea of having sex on a golf cart in the middle of a golf course is . . .

⬜ hot ⬜ warm ⬜ not especially interesting ⬜ out of the question

The idea of having sex in the back of a pickup truck is . . .

⬜ hot ⬜ warm ⬜ not especially interesting ⬜ out of the question

The idea of having sex in a hot air balloon is . . .

⬜ hot ⬜ warm ⬜ not especially interesting ⬜ out of the question

The idea of having sex in an actor's trailer on a movie set is . . .

⬜ hot ⬜ warm ⬜ not especially interesting ⬜ out of the question

PEEKABOO . . .

The idea of getting caught while having sex is . . .
⬜ exciting ⬜ horrible
⬜ only exciting if we don't actually get caught
⬜ only exciting if we do actually get caught

The idea of having sex in public is . . .
⬜ exciting ⬜ horrible
⬜ only exciting if we aren't actually seen
⬜ only exciting if we are actually seen

The idea of having sex in a closet during a party is . . .

⬜ hot ⬜ warm ⬜ not especially interesting ⬜ out of the question

The idea of having sex in a closet during work is . . .

⬜ hot ⬜ warm ⬜ not especially interesting ⬜ out of the question

The idea of having sex in a closet during Parents' Night at the local high school is . . .

☐ hot ☐ warm ☐ not especially interesting ☐ out of the question

The idea of having sex in a closet during a church social is . . .

☐ hot ☐ warm ☐ not especially interesting ☐ out of the question

The idea of having sex on a deserted beach is . . .

☐ hot ☐ warm ☐ not especially interesting ☐ out of the question

The idea of having sex on a crowded beach is . . .

☐ hot ☐ warm ☐ not especially interesting ☐ out of the question

The idea of having sex at a tourist attraction is . . .

☐ hot ☐ warm ☐ not especially interesting ☐ out of the question

The idea of having sex in a parked car on a deserted lovers' lane is . . .

☐ hot ☐ warm ☐ not especially interesting ☐ out of the question

The idea of having sex in a parked car in a crowded parking lot is . . .

☐ hot ☐ warm ☐ not especially interesting ☐ out of the question

The idea of having sex in a moving car is . . .

☐ hot ☐ warm ☐ not especially interesting ☐ out of the question

The idea of having sex in an elevator is . . .

☐ hot ☐ warm ☐ not especially interesting ☐ out of the question

The idea of having sex in a glass elevator is . . .

☐ hot ☐ warm ☐ not especially interesting ☐ out of the question

The idea of fondling under the table in a high-end restaurant is . . .

☐ hot ☐ warm ☐ not especially interesting ☐ out of the question

The idea of having sex in the middle of the stacks in a library is . . .

☐ hot ☐ warm ☐ not especially interesting ☐ out of the question

The idea of having sex in a hot tub is . . .

☐ hot ☐ warm ☐ not especially interesting ☐ out of the question

The idea of having sex in a hotel room where we can be overheard is . . .

☐ hot ☐ warm ☐ not especially interesting ☐ out of the question

The idea of having sex on the hotel balcony is . . .

☐ hot ☐ warm ☐ not especially interesting ☐ out of the question

The idea of having sex under my desk at work is . . .

☐ hot ☐ warm ☐ not especially interesting ☐ out of the question

The idea of having sex on my desk at work is . . .

☐ hot ☐ warm ☐ not especially interesting ☐ out of the question

The idea of having sex on the boss's desk at work is . . .

☐ hot ☐ warm ☐ not especially interesting ☐ out of the question

The idea of having sex on a mountaintop is . . .

☐ hot ☐ warm ☐ not especially interesting ☐ out of the question

The idea of having sex on a ski lift is . . .

☐ hot ☐ warm ☐ not especially interesting ☐ out of the question

The idea of having sex in the middle of a crowded dance club is . . .

☐ hot ☐ warm ☐ not especially interesting ☐ out of the question

A Touch of Kink

chapter 9

If You Don't Ask, You'll Never Know . . .

I've fantasized about incorporating leather gear into sex.

    ☐ yes ☐ no

I'd want to actually try it.

    ☐ yes, some of the time ☐ yes, all of the time
    ☐ no ☐ I don't know

I've fantasized about incorporating latex into sex.

    ☐ yes ☐ no

I'd want to actually try it.

    ☐ yes, some of the time ☐ yes, all of the time
    ☐ no ☐ I don't know

I've fantasized about incorporating foot worship into sex.

    ☐ yes ☐ no

I'd want to actually try it.

    ☐ yes, some of the time ☐ yes, all of the time
    ☐ no ☐ I don't know

I've fantasized about incorporating water sports into sex.

☐ yes ☐ no

I'd want to actually try it.

☐ yes, some of the time ☐ yes, all of the time
☐ no ☐ I don't know

I've fantasized about incorporating polyamory into my sex life.

☐ yes ☐ no

I'd want to actually try it.

☐ yes ☐ no ☐ I don't know

I've fantasized about incorporating Shibari (Japanese rope-tying) into my sex life.

☐ yes ☐ no

I'd want to actually try it.

☐ yes ☐ no ☐ I don't know

I've fantasized about incorporating Tantra into my sex life.

☐ yes ☐ no

I'd want to actually try it.

☐ yes ☐ no ☐ I don't know

I've fantasized about having sex with a consenting partner who is sleeping.

☐ yes ☐ no

I'd want to actually try it.

☐ yes ☐ no ☐ I don't know .

I've fantasized about someone having sex with me while I'm sleeping.

☐ yes ☐ no

I'd want to actually try it.

☐ yes ☐ no ☐ I don't know

I've fantasized about incorporating a collar or leash into my sex life.

☐ yes ☐ no

I'd want to actually try it.

☐ yes ☐ no ☐ I don't know

I've fantasized about incorporating cross-dressing into my sex life.

☐ yes ☐ no

I'd want to actually try it.

☐ yes ☐ no ☐ I don't know

I've fantasized about incorporating tongue piercing into my sex life.

☐ yes ☐ no

I'd want to actually try it.

☐ yes ☐ no ☐ I don't know

I've fantasized about incorporating genital piercing into my sex life.

☐ yes ☐ no

I'd want to actually try it.

☐ yes ☐ no ☐ I don't know

I've fantasized about incorporating animal role-play into my sex life.

☐ yes ☐ no

I'd want to actually try it.

☐ yes ☐ no ☐ I don't know

I've fantasized about incorporating performance as an inanimate object (e.g., acting as a footstool, sofa, ashtray, etc.) into my sex life.

☐ yes ☐ no

I'd want to actually try it.

☐ yes ☐ no ☐ I don't know

Sweet Dilemmas

chapter 10

I'd Rather Have . . .

- ☐ leather
- ☐ blindfold
- ☐ spanking
- ☐ endless teasing
- ☐ bonbons
- ☐ a caveman
- ☐ Tarzan
- ☐ a surgeon
- ☐ a cat person
- ☐ Bill Gates
- ☐ an operatic tenor
- ☐ a motorcycle
- ☐ silk sheets
- ☐ a satin gown
- ☐ a merman/mermaid
- ☐ wings
- ☐ a hippie
- ☐ a secluded weekend with my partner
- ☐ compelling eyes
- ☐ a whirlwind trip to Paris
- ☐ a back massage

- ☐ lace
- ☐ binoculars
- ☐ tickling
- ☐ a quickie
- ☐ thumbscrews
- ☐ a millionaire
- ☐ the boy next door
- ☐ a mechanic
- ☐ a dog person
- ☐ Indiana Jones
- ☐ a gangsta rapper
- ☐ a limousine
- ☐ a sleeping bag
- ☐ ripped jeans
- ☐ a centaur
- ☐ a tail
- ☐ a stockbroker
- ☐ a rowdy weekend with a water polo team
- ☐ a sexy voice
- ☐ an African safari
- ☐ a pillow fight

- [ ] a perfect body
- [ ] love 'em and leave 'em
- [ ] Prada heels
- [ ] sweet vanilla
- [ ] multiple orgasms
- [ ] a robot army
- [ ] a love potion
- [ ] a perfect behind
- [ ] missionary
- [ ] three sexy roommates
- [ ] a penthouse apartment
- [ ] an amazing body
- [ ] an astronaut
- [ ] the power of flight
- [ ] a vegan

- [ ] a brilliant mind
- [ ] spooning all night
- [ ] flip-flops
- [ ] spicy kink
- [ ] multiple partners
- [ ] a fairy godmother
- [ ] a Ph.D.
- [ ] perfect breasts/pecs
- [ ] reverse cowgirl
- [ ] one sexy doorman
- [ ] an Alpine cottage
- [ ] amazing bed skills
- [ ] a cave dweller
- [ ] the power to turn invisible
- [ ] a carnivore

I'd Rather Visit . . .

- [ ] the Middle Ages
- [ ] an enchanted forest
- [ ] Windsor Palace
- [ ] a football stadium
- [ ] a mermaid's garden
- [ ] a South American rain forest
- [ ] the hills of Ireland
- [ ] a speakeasy
- [ ] a literary salon
- [ ] a gladiator ring
- [ ] a hippie commune
- [ ] the backseat of a limousine
- [ ] the top of Everest
- [ ] the Egyptian pyramids
- [ ] Notre Dame
- [ ] the Arctic Circle
- [ ] the crew's quarters
- [ ] the day spa
- [ ] a yoga class
- [ ] a barbecue
- [ ] an Amish farm house

- [ ] outer space
- [ ] the beach
- [ ] a tent in the woods
- [ ] a secluded mountain retreat
- [ ] the mile-high club
- [ ] a desert oasis

- [ ] the streets of Hong Kong
- [ ] a disco
- [ ] a jai alai game
- [ ] a joust
- [ ] the floor of the stock market
- [ ] the cockpit of a jet

- [ ] the bottom of the ocean
- [ ] the Colorado Rockies
- [ ] the Arecibo Observatory
- [ ] the Equator
- [ ] the promenade deck
- [ ] the dungeon
- [ ] a rugby game
- [ ] a sushi bar
- [ ] a pool hall

- the Holodeck
- the AV club
- a Viking longship

- the open prairie
- detention
- a Hawaiian outrigger

I'd Rather Be . . .

- master
- princess
- harem girl
- watched
- the vampire
- a rock star
- a teacher
- an heir/heiress
- an Olympic athlete
- a Supreme Court justice
- an exotic dancer
- a gymnast
- a sorceress
- a professional gambler
- a 1950s housewife
- a great kisser
- a folk singer
- happy
- famous while I'm alive
- different
- perfect
- a hero

- servant
- saucy maid
- warrior queen
- the watcher
- the victim
- a groupie
- a student
- a self-made man/woman
- a ballerina
- a Playmate
- a naughty librarian
- a fighter pilot
- a CEO
- a master thief
- a 1920s flapper
- a sweet talker
- a concert violinist
- always right
- posthumously famous
- one of the gang
- flawed
- a villain

I'd Rather Star in . . .

- a historical bodice-ripper
- a screwball romantic comedy
- an action flick with lots of explosions
- a standard romantic comedy
- a teen sex comedy

- a spy game
- a cowboy movie
- an Edwardian romance
- an artsy European mindbender
- a gritty indie film

- ☐ a suspense thriller
- ☐ a Stooges slapstick
- ☐ a Gothic romance
- ☐ *Casablanca*
- ☐ a futuristic techno-thriller
- ☐ a swashbuckler
- ☐ a Pixar film
- ☐ a silent movie
- ☐ a Civil War miniseries
- ☐ an R-rated film
- ☐ a horror flick
- ☐ a heavy drama
- ☐ a punk-rock documentary
- ☐ *The English Patient*
- ☐ a swords-and-sorcery epic
- ☐ a sex-ed film
- ☐ a Japanese anime movie
- ☐ a 3-D flick
- ☐ a mystery
- ☐ a porn flick

THE OBJECT(S) OF MY AFFECTIONS

The most important thing about my fantasy partners is . . .

- ☐ the way they look
- ☐ the way they behave
- ☐ their level of passion

My ideal fantasy partner is . . .

- ☐ suave and cosmopolitan
- ☐ buttoned-down and professional
- ☐ a regular Joe or Jane six-pack
- ☐ a tattooed artist
- ☐ a barbarian
- ☐ an animal
- ☐ no, really, an animal

My fantasy partner . . .

- ☐ is silent
- ☐ whispers sweet nothings in my ear
- ☐ talks dirty to me

I'm most likely to fantasize about . . .

- ☐ my current partner ☐ ex-lovers
- ☐ old crushes ☐ friends ☐ coworkers
- ☐ celebrities ☐ people I've seen on the street
- ☐ completely made-up people

The celebrities I fantasize about are . . .

    ☐ politicians ☐ rock stars ☐ movie stars ☐ models
    ☐ other: _____

I'd rather be . . .

    ☐ the celebrity ☐ the fan

My fantasy partners are . . .

    ☐ openly affectionate ☐ distant

My fantasy partners offer me . . .

    ☐ freedom and spontaneity ☐ stability

My fantasy partners are . . .

    ☐ demure ☐ outspoken ☐ playful ☐ aggressive

My fantasy partners . . .

    ☐ dress outrageously ☐ dress to impress
    ☐ hide their sexiness under ordinary street clothes ☐ are naked

My fantasy partners are sexy because of . . .

    ☐ their bodies ☐ their minds ☐ their power
    ☐ their money ☐ their humor ☐ their talent

My fantasy partners' nether regions are . . .

    ☐ natural ☐ hairless ☐ somewhere in between

My fantasy partners are . . .

    ☐ heavily pierced and tattooed
    ☐ just a little of each ☐ unmarked

My fantasy partners are . . .

    ☐ smarter than I am ☐ less smart ☐ about the same

My fantasy partners are more likely to . . .

    ☐ admire me ☐ draw my admiration

My fantasy partners want me for my . . .

    ☐ body ☐ mind ☐ talent ☐ power ☐ humor
    ☐ other: _____

My fantasy partners' bodies are . . .

    ☐ muscular/tight from the gym
    ☐ muscular/tight from hard work
    ☐ muscular/tight from the outdoors
    ☐ soft/voluptuous
    ☐ slender
    ☐ big and beautiful
    ☐ androgynous

My fantasy partners . . .

    ☐ completely understand me
    ☐ are fascinated by my mystery

My fantasy partners . . .

    ☐ flirt shyly from afar
    ☐ entice me with gifts
    ☐ boldly proposition me
    ☐ just take me
    ☐ other: _____

My fantasy partners . . .

    ☐ are easy conquests
    ☐ need lots of seducing
    ☐ are faintly inappropriate conquests, such as:

_____

_____

My fantasy partners come to me . . .

    ☐ one at a time ☐ in pairs ☐ in groups

My fantasy partners . . .

☐ need to be tamed ☐ need to be loosened up

My fantasy partners are . . .

☐ compassionate ☐ ruthless ☐ changeable

My fantasy partners . . .

☐ inspire me to be better
☐ are inspired by me
☐ Honestly, we just inspire each other to get busy.

My fantasy partners are . . .

☐ lovers ☐ fighters ☐ thinkers ☐ jokers

My fantasy partners . . .

☐ energize me ☐ tire me out ☐ both, in that order

Set the Scene

A Figment of Your Imagination

My favorite office fantasy involves . . .

- [ ] the boss [ ] a peer
- [ ] a subordinate [ ] the courier man/woman

My office fantasy takes place . . .

- [ ] on the desk, after hours
- [ ] in the locked conference room, during a break
- [ ] under the desk, during work
- [ ] on the desk, during work

My favorite fairy-tale fantasy involves . . .

- [ ] being the prince- or damsel-in-distress
- [ ] doing the rescuing
- [ ] Who cares? Bring on the elves.

I'd rather . . .

- [ ] slay the dragon [ ] ride the dragon [ ] snog the dragon

Dungeons are for . . .

- [ ] spanking [ ] getting spanked
- [ ] hunting for goblin treasure [ ] someone else

My alpine ski fantasy involves . . .

- ☐ multiple hotties in cute outfits
- ☐ some very special one-on-one ski lessons
- ☐ having to find some way to stay warm with a stranger after an avalanche
- ☐ a romantic evening by the fire with my partner

I'd rather . . .

- ☐ be the ski student
- ☐ do the expert instructing
- ☐ I told you: We're not leaving the lodge.

The fantasy where I'm working at a suitably large desk and feel someone underneath parting my knees to start pleasuring me takes place . . .

- ☐ in front of my college English students
- ☐ in my empty office after work
- ☐ in my Vice President's office, as I'm giving instructions to a subordinate
- ☐ in the Oval Office, as I'm addressing the nation

My vampire fantasy involves . . .

- ☐ joining the handsome count or beautiful countess in undeath
- ☐ getting rescued by a dashing vampire hunter
- ☐ doing the rescuing
- ☐ being the vampire

My favorite camping fantasy involves . . .

- ☐ sex under the stars with my partner
- ☐ meeting some sexy hikers on a suitably lonely path
- ☐ livening up the ranger station
- ☐ staying in the tent all day and night

My tropical island fantasy involves . . .

- ☐ a luxury resort
- ☐ a thatch hut on the beach
- ☐ a yacht
- ☐ being shipwrecked with a hot sailor

My gym fantasy involves . . .

- ☐ the sauna ☐ the weight machines
- ☐ the showers ☐ a full aerobics class

My car wash fantasy involves . . .

    ☐ me in the tight, wet T-shirt ☐ me in the car ☐ me as the car

My Wild West fantasy involves . . .

    ☐ building a homestead with my partner
    ☐ cleaning up the town with the good guys/gals
    ☐ shooting up the town with the bad guys/gals
    ☐ never leaving the saloon

My palatial mansion fantasy involves . . .

    ☐ "training" the servants
    ☐ being the servant
    ☐ showing my shy new betrothed each and every one of the 36 bedrooms

My space adventure fantasy involves . . .

    ☐ the tension of spending days in a cabin with my hot first mate
    ☐ discovering an entire alien race that's madly attracted to me
    ☐ The Pleasurebot 5000

My mad scientist fantasy involves . . .

    ☐ discovering the perfect love potion
    ☐ creating the perfect mate
    ☐ whipping off my glasses so that the entire Nobel Peace Prize committee suddenly sees how sexy I am

Choose Your Own Ending

You're fresh out of the bath in a luxury hotel in a foreign city. You're just taking a sensual moment to put on some scented lotion, when suddenly you get the sense that someone is watching you through a gap in the curtains.

    ☐ You put on a show.
    ☐ You invite your new friend inside.
    ☐ You call the sexy hotel manager to get rid of the creep, then figure out a special way to say "thank you."
    ☐ other: _____

_____

_____

_____

You're on a secluded beach, looking fabulous in your new bathing suit.

- ☐ You seduce the sexy lifeguard.
- ☐ You seduce several sexy lifeguards.
- ☐ You frolic in the surf with your partner.
- ☐ You offer to rub some lotion on the back of the beautiful man or woman on the next blanket.
- ☐ other: _____

_____

_____

Pirates! They overtake your small sailboat and you're captured!

- ☐ You become the Captain's special thrall.
- ☐ You entertain the entire crew.
- ☐ You take over the ship and do a little plundering.
- ☐ other: _____

_____

_____

You're on a road trip and stop in a seedy country bar. You seduce . . .

- ☐ the rugged cowboy/cowgirl
- ☐ the grimy biker
- ☐ the sweet-natured busboy/busgirl
- ☐ the tart-tongued bartender
- ☐ other: _____

_____

_____

You're exploring new territory in the deepest jungle, and supplies are running out.

- ☐ You find a new treetop city with your hot guide.
- ☐ You contract a fever and are nursed back to health by extremely friendly natives.
- ☐ You stumble onto a fabulous lost treasure and return home to a life of luxury with your surprisingly attractive assistant.
- ☐ other: _____

_____

_____

You're a master cat burglar, silently prowling the rooftops of the rich.

- ☐ You leave mysterious gifts to seduce an attractive stranger.
- ☐ You're caught and explain you'll do just about anything to mollify the attractive homeowner.
- ☐ You steal as many kisses as you do jewels but don't settle down with anyone.
- ☐ other: _____

_____

_____

You're a firebrand in revolutionary France. Society is changing. Paris is burning.

- ☐ You have a forbidden affair with an aristocrat.
- ☐ You fall in love with a fellow revolutionary while you're storming the Bastille.
- ☐ Politics schmolitics, it's all about ripping off those sexy outfits.
- ☐ other: _____

_____

_____

It's your first semester on your new college campus, and you're eager to find new friends.

- ☐ You earn an enthusiastic A from your creative writing professor.
- ☐ You learn that your new roommate has a few surprises in store.
- ☐ The entire drama department asks you to take a bow.
- ☐ other: _____

_____

_____

Your flight has been unexpectedly grounded and you'll have to spend the night in a strange city.

- ☐ You share a hotel room with the hottie from first class.
- ☐ You find out that the flight crew really does give service with a smile.
- ☐ You fly a small, private plane out with a grateful copilot.
- ☐ other: _____

_____

_____

Past and Future Fantasies

chapter **12**

The Pleasure of Fantasy

What is your favorite fantasy right now?

_____

_____

_____

What was your favorite fantasy as a teenager?

_____

_____

_____

Do you still find it sexy?

☐ yes ☐ no

How do you think your past fantasy influenced your current fantasies or love life?

_____

_____

_____

How do you think you're different in the way you fantasize now?

_____

_____

_____

What were your favorite books or stories when you were young?

_____

_____

How do you think they have influenced your fantasy life?

_____

_____

_____

Why do you think your current favorite fantasies are your favorites?

_____

_____

_____

How do you think your fantasies have helped you grow sexually?

_____

_____

_____

How do you think your fantasies have helped you grow as a person?

_____

_____

_____

Which past crush has had the biggest influence on your fantasies?

_____

Why?

_____

_____

Which partner has had the biggest influence on your fantasies?

_____

Why?

_____

_____

Which person in your life has been the biggest inhibitor of your fantasies?

_____

Why?

_____

_____

Which person (other than you) has had the biggest hand in helping them blossom?

_____

Why?

_____

_____

What is the biggest difference between you in your fantasies and you in real life?

_____

_____

What keeps you from being more like the fantasy you?

_____

_____

Not All Fantasies Are About Sex

I fantasize about my real life having more adventure in it.
☐ true ☐ false

I fantasize about my real life having more love in it.
☐ true ☐ false

I fantasize about my real life having more friends in it.
☐ true ☐ false

I fantasize about my real life having more creativity in it.
☐ true ☐ false

I fantasize about my real life having more laughter in it.
☐ true ☐ false

I fantasize about my real life having more fun in it.
☐ true ☐ false

I fantasize about having more money.
☐ true ☐ false

I fantasize about having a better job.
☐ true ☐ false

I fantasize about being more outgoing.
☐ true ☐ false

I fantasize about being more mysterious.
☐ true ☐ false

I fantasize about being more playful.
☐ true ☐ false

I fantasize about being more adult.
☐ true ☐ false

I fantasize about being more open to new experiences.
☐ true ☐ false

I fantasize about being more assertive.
☐ true ☐ false

I fantasize about being better educated.
☐ true ☐ false

I fantasize about being more elegant.
☐ true ☐ false

I fantasize about being more athletic.
☐ true ☐ false

I fantasize about being more spiritual.
☐ true ☐ false

I fantasize about taking more risks.
☐ true ☐ false

I fantasize about being a rock star.
☐ true ☐ false

I fantasize about being an actor.
☐ true ☐ false

I fantasize about being an artist.
☐ true ☐ false

I fantasize about being a designer.
☐ true ☐ false

I fantasize about being a writer.
☐ true ☐ false

I fantasize about being a doctor.

☐ true ☐ false

I fantasize about being a scientist.

☐ true ☐ false

I fantasize about being a teacher.

☐ true ☐ false

I fantasize about running for office.

☐ true ☐ false

I fantasize about being a police officer.

☐ true ☐ false

I fantasize about being an international spy.

☐ true ☐ false

I fantasize about working outdoors.

☐ true ☐ false

Actually, I fantasize most about being:

_____

_____

I fantasize about quitting my job and traveling the world.

☐ true ☐ false

I fantasize about living overseas.

☐ true ☐ false

I fantasize about learning another language.

☐ true ☐ false

I fantasize about learning a new craft or skill.

    ☐ true   ☐ false

I fantasize about doing more volunteer work.

    ☐ true   ☐ false

I fantasize about spending more time with my family.

    ☐ true   ☐ false

I fantasize about having more time to myself.

    ☐ true   ☐ false

I fantasize about learning to hang glide or skydive.

    ☐ true   ☐ false

I fantasize about being single.

    ☐ true   ☐ false

I fantasize about getting married.

    ☐ true   ☐ false

I fantasize about having kids.

    ☐ true   ☐ false

I fantasize about telling off my boss.

    ☐ true   ☐ false

I fantasize about getting rid of toxic friends.

    ☐ true   ☐ false

Here's what I fantasize about that hasn't been covered:

_____

_____

_____

_____

Here's how I think I could move closer to my fantasy life:

_____

_____

_____

Here's what I'm going to do this week to get closer to my fantasies:

_____

_____

_____

Here's what I'm going to do this month to get closer to my fantasies:

_____

_____

_____

Here's what I'm going to do this year to get closer to my fantasies:

_____

_____

_____

Here's what I'm going to do over the next five years to make my fantasies come true:

_____

_____

_____

_____

ABOUT THE AUTHOR

Kate F. Moore has worked as a freelance writer and copyeditor for more than ten years. She has performed one-woman shows in Chicago, New York, Edinburgh, and Los Angeles. Kate lives (and fantasizes) in New York, NY.